BELUGA
WHALES

Printed in Hong Kong

96   97   98   99   00   5   4   3   2   1

Library of Congress Cataloging-in-Publication Data

Martin, Anthony, 1954–
    Beluga whales / by Anthony Martin.
        p.   cm. — (WorldLife library)
    Includes bibliographical references (p.72)
    ISBN 0-89658-306-6
    1. White whale.   I. Title.   II. Series.
QL737.C433M37   1996
599.5'3—dc20   95-5922
                                                                    CIP

Published by Voyageur Press, Inc.
123 North Second Street, P.O. Box 338, Stillwater, MN 55082 U.S.A.
612-430-2210, fax 612-430-2211

*Please write or call, or stop by, for our free catalog of natural history publications. Our toll-free
number to place an order or to obtain a free catalog is 800-888-WOLF (800-888-9653).*

Educators, fundraisers, premium and gift buyers, publicists, and marketing managers:
Looking for creative products and new sales ideas? Voyageur Press books are available at special
discounts when purchased in quantities, and special editions can be created to your
specifications. For details contact the marketing department.

Photography Copyright © 1996 by:

Front cover © Gunter Ziesler (Bruce Coleman)
Back cover © Doug Allan
Page   1 © Doug Allan
Page   4 © Tony Martin
Page   6 © Flip Nicklin (Minden Pictures)
Page   8 © Tony Martin
Page   9 © Gunter Ziesler (Bruce Coleman)
Page 10 © Doug Allan
Page 13 © Tony Martin
Page 14 © Tony Martin (Oxford Scientific Films)
Page 16 © Tony Martin
Page 17 © Tony Martin
Page 18 © Tony Martin
Page 19 © Doug Allan
Page 21 © Flip Nicklin (Minden Pictures)
Page 22 © Doug Allan
Page 23 © Tony Martin

Page 24 © Tony Martin
Page 25 © Doud Allan
Page 26 © Gunter Ziesler (Bruce Coleman)
Page 29 © Tony Martin
Page 31 © Doug Allan
Page 32 © Tony Martin
Page 34 © Doug Allan (Oxford Scientific Films)
Page 35 © Tony Martin
Page 36 © Tony Martin
Page 39 © Tony Martin
Page 41 © Tony Martin
Page 42 © Doug Allan (Oxford Scientific Films)
Page 45 © Tony Martin
Page 46 © Gunter Ziesler (Bruce Coleman)
Page 49 © Tony Martin
Page 50 © Doug Allan (Oxford Scientific Films)
Page 51 © Doug Allan

Page 52 © Frans Lanting (Minden Pictures)
Page 53 © Doug Allan
Page 55 © Lothar Dahlke
Page 56 © Tony Martin
Page 59 © David Fleetham (Oxford Scientific Films)
Page 60 © Wyb Hoek (Marine Mammal Images)
Page 61 © Tony Martin
Page 62 © Tony Martin (Oxford Scientific Films)
Page 63 © Doug Allan (Oxford Scientific Films)
Page 64 © Tony Martin
Page 67 © Tony Martin
Page 68 © Tony Martin
Page 69 © Tony Martin
Page 70 © Tony Martin
Page 71 © Doug Allan (Oxford Scientific Films)

BELUGA
WHALES

Tony Martin

Voyageur Press

Contents

Introduction

Even among the extraordinary group of creatures that we call cetaceans – whales, dolphins and porpoises – the white whale or beluga is a remarkable and striking animal. Historically, it was known in the wild to only the hardy residents and explorers of the far north. They usually encountered belugas for a brief period in summer and could not know that the whales' sudden appearance and disappearance was due to a migratory cycle that might cover thousands of miles each year. Today, because of the increasing number of tourists venturing to previously inaccessible colder climes, and the beluga's adaptability to captivity, it is to many a familiar animal. Nonetheless, even now, more than 200 years after it was first described, no-one can claim to fully understand the way of life of this unique creature. As we shall see, modern and sophisticated research methods are beginning to unlock its secrets, but each answer spawns yet more questions, and we are still a long way from knowing even some of the most fundamental things about it.

My own particular interest in the beluga stemmed from a memorable film sequence in Sir David Attenborough's 'Living Planet' series of BBC television documentaries. It started with a close-up of Attenborough talking to camera, then the lens pulled slowly back to reveal that he was standing within a few yards of a large group of pure white whales. They were splashing and cavorting in shallow water, apparently oblivious to the close human presence and making a great deal of noise. Already an addict of the Arctic, having been to the region as a young whale biologist on several occasions, I resolved there and then to see this amazing spectacle for myself. In one of those strange quirks of fate, the opportunity arose within a few years when Dr Tom Smith, the Canadian scientist whose camp Attenborough had stayed in to film the sequence, visited my laboratory in Cambridge, England. Over a beer in a local pub we put together a joint research project which combined Tom's unrivaled knowledge of high Arctic belugas with my own work in the rapidly developing field of radio tracking. Tom's fieldcamp is in Cunningham Inlet on the north coast of Somerset Island, part of Canada's new territory of Nunavut. The Inlet overlooks the fabled Northwest Passage which claimed the lives of so many British sailors in the 18th century when this region was being explored. It is a pristine and extremely striking environment, leaving an indelible mark on those privileged to

A typical summer scene in Cunningham Inlet.

go there. This is where I first saw belugas and have spent most time with them. As such, it is to me a very special place, and much of my understanding of this animal stems from the many summers I have spent there with Tom. The Cunningham Inlet project was the start of a research program which has led to me studying belugas in many parts of the Arctic every year since 1987. What started as intrigue has led to a passion to learn more and more about this fascinating creature, and to following it, one way or another, to every country where it occurs.

The idea for this book grew and took shape over a number of years, usually while sitting in a tent or hut, watching and marveling at belugas in a remote Arctic estuary. What follows is a portrayal of the whale itself, what is known about it and how man has interacted with it over the centuries. The text largely reflects a personal perspective, built up over many years of studying this animal, but I pay tribute here to the scientists, hunters and naturalists whose contribution to knowledge has made such a book possible.

An aerial view of Canada's Cunningham River estuary.

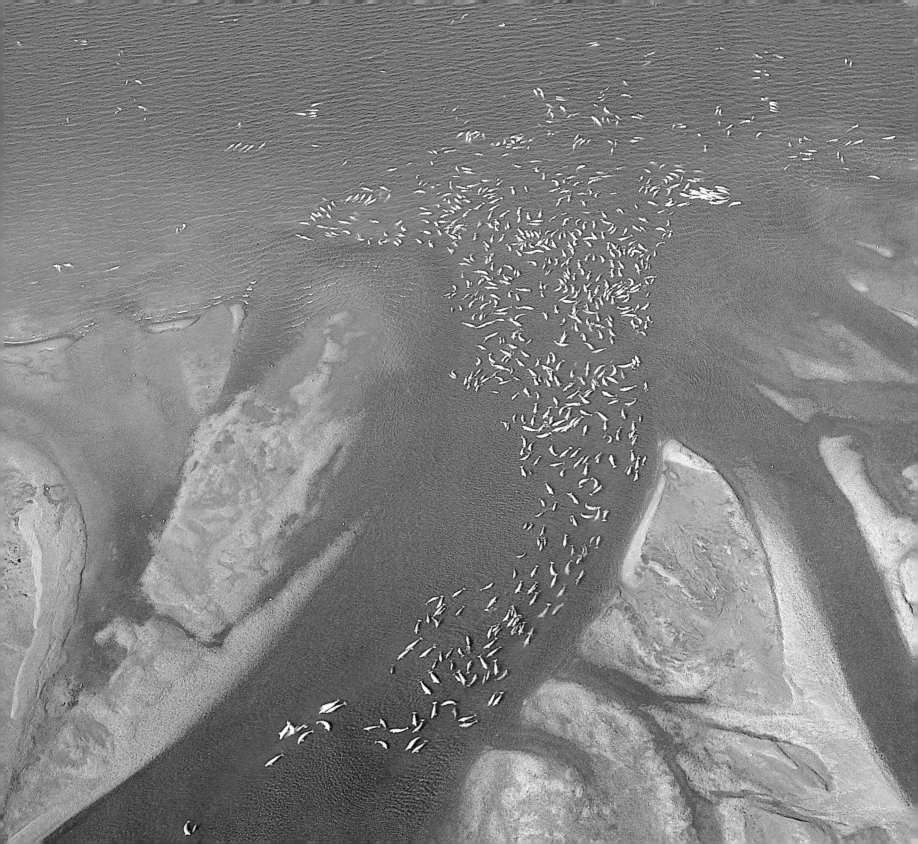

What is a Beluga?

Belugas, and all cetaceans, are mammals. We believe that they have evolved from a land-based animal which may have resembled today's ungulates (cows, deer, etc) and which began to adopt an increasingly aquatic existence around 50 million years ago. Animals that we would recognize as whales or dolphins certainly existed 25 million years ago, but the earliest fossils of creatures recognizably similar to the modern-day beluga are from the Miocene, about 10 million years ago. These have been discovered in California and Mexico, indicating that adaptation to the current, purely Arctic range of the family must have occurred relatively recently.

Some 80 species of whales, dolphins and porpoises are known to exist today. Together they form a distinctive group of creatures which scientists recognize as an Order, the *cetacea*. Despite these similarities, they nevertheless vary in size, form and lifestyle to an extraordinary degree. The largest, the blue whale, is more than 1,000 times heavier than the smallest dolphins and porpoises. Most species in the group, the beluga among them, have teeth and capture their prey individually. In contrast, most of the largest whales harvest swarms of their food (usually plankton) from the ocean with a sieve-like structure in their mouths called baleen. Some species occur almost throughout the world, while others are restricted to relatively tiny areas. Some can only survive in tropical waters and others, like the beluga, are found exclusively in cold seas. Most are marine in habit yet, extraordinarily, a few (the river dolphins) spend their whole lives in fresh water, often thousands of miles from the sea.

Among this bewildering variety, the beluga can be considered a small whale, with a maximum body weight of some two tons and maximum body length of around 18 ft (5.5 m). Its scientific name *Delphinapterus leucas* literally means 'white dolphin without a wing' (meaning without a dorsal fin) and indeed its color distinguishes it from all other whales or dolphins. Common names of 'white whale' and 'beluga' are equally used in the English language, the latter being a corruption of *belukha* which is the Russian name for this creature. The beluga is closely related to one other living cetacean, the narwhal, with which it shares a taxonomic family (*Monodontidae*). Until recently, some scientists considered that the Irrawaddy Dolphin (*Orcaella brevirostris*) should be placed in this family, but genetic evidence now indicates that this species is more closely related to the marine dolphins, despite many outward similarities to the beluga. Adult male belugas are always larger than adult females in the same population (by some 16-24% in length) and different populations vary considerably in body size. As an example, males occurring in northern Quebec are typically only around 75% of the length and 60% of the weight of those swimming off west Greenland. An 'average' female beluga will be in the range 10-12 ft (3.1-3.7 m) in length and 900-1,400 lb (408-627 kg) in weight, whereas males average around 12-15 ft (3.6-4.5 m) and 1,340-2,275 lb (607-1,032 kg) respectively.

Surprisingly, not all white whales are white, and even the white ones don't appear white all year round! Calves are born gray-brown in color, and at a length of about 4 ft, 6 in-5 ft, 3 in (1.4-1.6 m). During the first few years of life they change to a dark blue-gray then become progressively lighter in color. Finally, between 4 and 15 years of age, depending on which population they come from, they lose any remaining tinge of grayness (except on the very top of the dorsal ridge and perhaps around the edges of the tail and pectoral fins) and assume the adult color of white. The story doesn't end there, though, because belugas are probably unique among cetaceans in that they undergo an intense period of molt each summer. In doing so, they lose their old outer skin (epidermis) layer, which has by this time become yellow, and regain their pure whiteness. The whale hastens the molt by rubbing itself on gravel or sand, usually in shallow fresh water, and it was this activity that was filmed in Cunningham Inlet for 'Living Planet'. There is evidence that immersion in fresh water may help the molt process, so rubbing on the bed of estuaries like Cunningham Inlet, or the

Belugas in the shallow, tidal waters of Elwin Bay on Canada's Somerset Island.
The muddy trails are left by whales rubbing on the bottom substrate.

Like the other truly Arctic whale species, Belugas have no dorsal fin.

Mackenzie delta in western Canada, may have a double benefit. Although rubbing has been recorded in wild killer whales, the beluga is the only cetacean which does it as intensely, in such large social groups and as spectacularly as the scene which stimulated my original interest in the white whale.

Belugas are by no means the most sleek of whales, and have a relatively rotund and robust shape unsuited to fast swimming. Unlike most other cetaceans, they are not even very rounded in cross-section; bulges and ridges give them an appearance of obesity which, as it happens, is not far from the truth. Their heads are quite square and blunt in shape and, unusually for whales, they have a discontinuity in outline between the head and thorax, resembling a marked 'neck'. As in all toothed whales, the forehead comprises an oil-filled organ called the 'melon'. In belugas, this is quite soft to the touch and its shape can be altered by the whale, changing its facial 'expression'. This characteristic may be linked with 'mood', for example to display aggression or appeasement. But the cetacean melon is normally considered to play a role in echolocation, the ability to detect objects by bouncing pulses of sound off them, and this is probably its primary function.

Like all cetaceans, belugas have a horizontal tail to provide forward movement and a pectoral fin or flipper on each side for stability and changing direction. A strange characteristic of the pectoral fins, shared only with the narwhal, is that they progressively turn up at the tip as the animal ages. As a result, the oldest whales, especially bulls, have 'J' shaped fins. There is no apparent function for this trait. In common only with the right whales, the right whale dolphins, the Irrawaddy dolphin and the narwhal, belugas have no dorsal fin (the vertical structure on the back which is most accentuated in killer whales). Instead, belugas possess a rather tough ridge on the mid-line of their back which may be used to break thin sea-ice and allow the animal to breathe. It is surely no coincidence that all three of the world's truly Arctic whales (the beluga, narwhal and bowhead) lack a dorsal fin, and we may therefore presume that life in ice-laden seas is easier without one. This may be because of unacceptable heat loss or because a fin would be vulnerable to ice damage. Of course, this begs the question as to why the two right whale dolphins and the Irrawaddy dolphin, which never encounter ice, also lack a fin. The answer to this puzzle may lie in their evolutionary history or it may indicate that in some circumstances the benefit of having the stability provided by a fin is outweighed by its disadvantages,

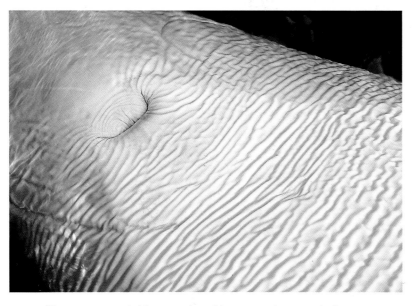

Transverse wrinkles on the skin are unique to belugas.

e.g. the increased drag and maintenance cost. In common only with the narwhal, the tail changes shape with age. In youngsters it has a fairly straight trailing edge, broken only by the notch in the middle, but by adulthood it is beautifully curvaceous.

To the touch, belugas have mostly a soft and smooth skin, but tight ridges across the line of the body often cover part of the thorax and upper abdomen, in the summer at least. The function of these ridges has not been explained, and they occur in few other cetaceans. They may be related to drag reduction, perhaps by minimizing turbulence, or may simply be a physical response to the seasonal immersion in fresh water.

Although the beluga shares many characteristics with its close cousin the narwhal, there are some important differences in the structure of the head and neck which reflect their different lifestyles. The most obvious is that belugas lack the famous single tusk, source of the unicorn myths, carried by adult male

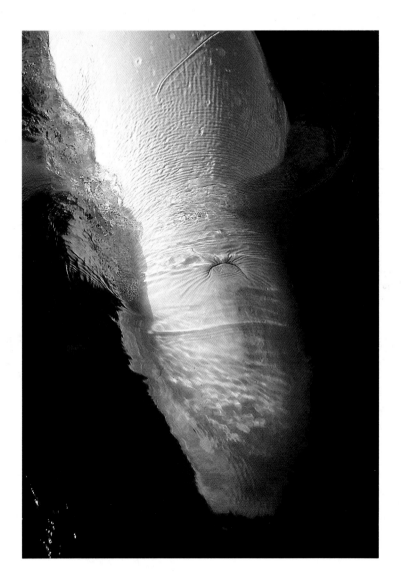

This whale still retains its old, yellow skin.
Within a few weeks it will be sloughed off and the animal
will become gleaming white once more.

narwhals. This tusk is what biologists call a 'secondary sexual characteristic', an adornment emphasizing maleness, similar to antlers in deer and beards in our own species. Such extravagant and unwieldy headgear carries a cost, though, and in the narwhal this includes a strengthening and rigidity of the neck vertebrae to cope with the considerable extra weight of the head and the tendency for it to be pulled to the left because the tusk is situated off-center. Not having a tusk, belugas require no strengthening of the neck and in fact have greater side-to-side flexibility in this region than most whales.

*The upturned pectoral fin of the beluga
to the right signifies that it is mature.*

Another difference between these two species is in the mouth. Narwhals have a small mouth opening and no erupted teeth except the tusk (which is not used for feeding, contrary to apocryphal stories that it is used to spear fish). In contrast, belugas have around 34 simple peg-like teeth in a large mouth that can open wide and be quickly clamped shut as occasional bruises on my legs during marking work have testified. Both sexes carry teeth, and they probably play a role in feeding, although this is often not the case in other whale species. As the narwhal, a 'toothed' whale, demonstrates, the lack of teeth in the mouth is no barrier to catching sufficient prey to make a living. Nevertheless, the number, size and shape of teeth are clues to the *type* of food taken. Even without any other evidence we might suspect that belugas and narwhals have evolved to specialize on different prey although they share much

Belugas are inquisitive creatures, here investigating the photographer.
The neck crease is obvious in this view.

the same habitat preference and have a dietary overlap.

Although male belugas do not differ from the females in such an obvious way as they do in narwhals, there are characteristics which distinguish them, especially in adulthood. One of these, apparently more accentuated in some beluga populations than others, is longitudinal ridges in the blubber below the midline which give large males an almost flat belly and chest. Another is that in adult males the head is proportionally longer and broader, and the shoulders more robust than in females, combined with an overall larger and heavier body. These characteristics together result in mature males appearing as very different animals to their female counterparts. This is known as sexual dimorphism and, as we shall see later in this book, may provide clues to the social and mating system operating in beluga populations.

The ability to survive the harsh Arctic environment has been brought about by both physical and behavioral adaptation. Physically, the most obvious cold-adapted attribute is the thick layer of blubber which covers everything except the extremities (head, tail and pectoral fins) and acts as a warm overcoat, giving belugas a very tubby appearance. Those parts of the body not covered in this padding appear disproportionately small. The head, in particular, may look like it is a mis-match to the rest of the whale. The blubber, which is unusually thick in this species (typically 1-3 in/25-75 mm) comprises oils and fats in a fibrous matrix and acts as a very effective insulating barrier between the core of the body at around 98.6°F (37°C) and the water, which can be below 32°F (0°C). Although the blubber layer of calves at birth is much thinner, the mother rapidly provides the youngster with material to build it up by producing extremely rich and fatty milk. This contains as much as 27% fat, compared to around 4% in cows' milk. Nevertheless, the ability of the newborn calf to survive the thermal shock of birth, transferring rapidly from the warmth and comfort of the mother's body to literally icy water, is amazing.

Patterns of Life

The beluga is a very social whale, rarely occurring alone and often associating with thousands of others. Groups of belugas, as with all cetaceans, are known as 'pods'. We believe that pod membership and size in belugas is unstable, i.e. that individuals often move between pods. This has been demonstrated in many ways, but most graphically to me when two whales from a single pod have been tracked using small radio transmitters. In most cases, the whales have followed separate paths within a few days and can be hundreds or even thousands of miles apart after a surprisingly short time. There have been two exceptions: an adult and sub-adult which were probably mother and son and, on another occasion, two adult males. The presumed mother/son case was fascinating, because the male, although still slightly gray and therefore immature, was actually longer than the female and probably five or six years old. The two whales were trapped together in a tidal pool, tagged, and subsequently tracked for more than 600 miles (1,000 km) during which time their paths overlapped entirely. They returned to the tagging site, Cunningham Inlet, two weeks after their involuntary entrapment and I was delighted to watch them through a telescope as they cavorted in the Cunningham River, clearly very closely bonded. This episode indicated for the first time that the mother-calf relationship can last for many years and may explain why adult females and their new-born calves are often associated with a third, immature beluga. This is probably the previous calf, which would normally become independent during the first year of life of the mother's next offspring, but may exceptionally remain in their mother's company for five or six years.

By piecing together evidence like this we get a picture of a species in which the mother/calf bond is probably the central relationship. Most frequently, numbers of mothers and their calf or calves form distinct groupings, as do adult males and sometimes other sections of the population, such as adult females without calves and weaned sub-adults. This was clearly the case on my first trip to Svalbard, when I saw hundreds of white animals, but not one adult male or youngster. Dark, and therefore young, animals had been seen in nearby fjords, but the area in which I was working held only a segment of the population. Similarly, in Cunningham Inlet, thousands of miles to the west, groups of exclusively adult males are often very obvious, their large heads and broad backs differentiating them from all other age- and sex-classes. The area may hold 1,000 animals of all sizes at the time, but most seek out others similar to themselves. A careful look across the inlet reveals that this large assembly of whales has a relatively fine structure, comprising many groups of between two and 30 animals which circulate as discrete units.

Belugas are very social whales, usually appearing in dense groups of tens to thousands

Much of our knowledge of the life history of belugas is incomplete, due largely to the species' inaccessibility for much of the year. Nevertheless, information gained from the examination of hunted animals and those held in captivity has allowed many pieces of the puzzle to be put together. For the remainder, we must rely on indirect evidence and analogy with other, better known, species for a 'best guess' at how populations of this whale function. Belugas are first able to reproduce at an age of about four to seven years in females and six to nine in males. Ovulating females probably mate with a different partner each cycle, and likely with several partners during

Adult males in Cunningham Inlet. Tight groups like this very often comprise animals of the same sex and maturity.

Calves are always born singly, and very dark in color.
Here, a youngster in its first month of life swims almost on its mother's back.
It will remain in close contact with her for at least two years.

each. Judging by the appearance of new-born calves, we believe that mating occurs quite synchronously across the population, probably in spring or early summer. Unfortunately, very few belugas are seen at this time of year, so no observations of their social or mating behavior at this critical time are available. The gestation period has variously been estimated at between 12 and 14 months. Calves are always produced singly, at intervals of two to four years, most often three years. The interval between births probably increases with the age of the mother, and pregnancy in older females may be rare. Fathers take no part in the rearing of their offspring, and may never encounter them.

Few beluga births have been witnessed in the wild, but a Canadian colleague and friend of mine, Jack Orr, was lucky enough to be in the right place at the right time one July. Looking down from a cliff top in aptly named Clearwater Fjord, Baffin Island, he witnessed the birth of a calf. The youngster was then apparently helped to the surface and supported by some of the small group of adults which had been standing nearby. Such 'helpers' have been observed at births of other whale species, and are often thought or known to be female relatives of the mother. This is unlikely to be the case for belugas because this whale does not form stable groups of related individuals as do, for example, killer whales and pilot whales. It may simply be that nearby adults, attracted by the calls of a female about to give birth, act as volunteer 'midwives'. If this behavior was normal within the population, all would benefit in the long term.

Sufficient belugas have now been born in captivity for us to know that, unusually for cetaceans, calves can leave the security of the mother's body either head- or tail-first. The umbilical cord snaps as the calf is finally and suddenly expelled into its new world. Over a period of days or weeks the remnants of the cord, its purpose achieved, fall away from the calf when the navel has healed. Apart from the umbilicus, newly born calves can be recognized by having a few light-colored vertical lines on their flanks which contrast with the otherwise dark body. These are called fetal folds and, as their name implies, are due to the youngster being curled up within the mother's uterus. They gradually disappear within a few months of birth.

Like all mammals, beluga mothers provide milk for their offspring in a process called lactation. They have two teats, which are situated in slits in the blubber on each side of the genital opening. Here, they are protected and do not disturb the flow of water over the whale's body, but can be exposed when a calf wants to suckle. The thick, fatty milk, which is often green in colour, must somehow be passed on to the calf without being wasted or diluted in the process. Nursing cannot be closely observed in the wild, but captive conditions allow us to watch the process from the newborn's first fumbling attempts to locate the nipple right through to weaning. Sometimes puffs of milk can be seen emanating from the nipple just after the youngster has lost contact with it, and it is clear that the mother can squirt the milk rather than simply rely on the calf sucking it in.

The youngster grows very rapidly on its rich diet. Nevertheless, unlike seals, which also grow fast and usually become independent of their mothers in a few weeks, belugas continue to nurse for more than a year. Solid food is probably taken for the first time at around six months and slowly becomes more important in the diet. Pregnant females may simultaneously be suckling the previous calf, but by this time relatively little milk is being provided and the mother needs to devote energy to the youngster growing within her.

We can determine the age of belugas by counting layers of dentine and cementum laid down in the teeth as they grow, much in the same way as trees can be aged by their rings. The layers are apparent because material added to the teeth varies seasonally, both in the core (the dentine) and the outer covering of the tooth, called the cementum. This species is unusual among toothed whales, though, in that two pairs of layers are deposited each year rather than just one. Even with our ability to judge their age, comparatively few belugas have been examined in this way. Very little information is yet available on the age structure of beluga populations, that is, the relative number of

A group of adult females, many of which have calves in close attendance.
The mother/calf relationship is probably the only long-lasting association in beluga society.

animals of each age class. What we do know suggests that this is not a long-lived species, and few whales live to 30 years. A 40-year-old is truly exceptional and might be equated with a centenarian in our own species. Males probably have a shorter life expectancy than females, and become sexually mature later as we have seen, but of course once mature they may father many calves each year. By analogy with other mammals with sexual dimorphism and no parental care in males, we might expect great variation in the success with which individuals are able to pass their genes on to the next generation.

An important measure of any wild animal population, especially if we are to evaluate the impact of a given level of hunting, is its potential rate of increase, i.e. the excess of births over deaths. Estimating this for whales is notoriously difficult, mainly because of the complexities of counting them accurately. To make matters worse, we should expect that it will differ both between different populations and even for any one population over time. Controversy has surrounded the calculation of this value for belugas because an unrealistically low estimate means that hunting communities will face lower-than-necessary quotas, while one which is too high can result in over-hunting and a consequent population crash. Perhaps the best estimate of this measure for any belugas is one of around 3% for the depleted St Lawrence population since the ending of hunting in 1979. The population has been monitored since that time, but even here some doubt remains about its status. To put the three per cent figure into context, such an increase would lead to a doubling every 20 years, but a population of 500 whales would start to decline with only 18 additional deaths a year due, say, to a disease outbreak.

A calf takes a look above water. This youngster will become progressively lighter with age, but the whiteness of adulthood takes many years to achieve.

Distribution and Abundance

Belugas occur only in the colder waters of the northern hemisphere, and more or less in a continuous band around the pole. All are familiar with sea ice, and many populations stay in ice-strewn waters all year round. Indeed, the seasonal encroachment and withdrawal of the Arctic ice blanket is a major influence on the lives of all belugas. Most white whales spend at least the summer months above the Arctic circle, an imaginary line around the globe at about latitude 66°30'N. However, because of climatic and oceanographic variations, places above the line (as in northern Norway) can have milder weather and warmer seas than others which are much further south, such as in Canada's Hudson's Bay. As a result, belugas can be found at latitudes from 46°N to at least 83°N, depending on both the season and the region they live in.

The North Pole, and most of the Arctic Ocean in which it lies, is covered with a blanket of sea ice. Until recently, this thick ice was thought to be impenetrable by sea mammals. However, sightings of ringed seals in the wake of ice-breaking ships at the pole itself, and the ability to track animals across this white desert using satellites passing unseen high overhead, have now shown us how wrong we were. Polar bears routinely venture out hundreds of miles from land over the polar pack-ice and some of my tagged belugas have also penetrated deep into ice-covered waters. Nevertheless, few belugas are likely to spend large amounts of time in continuous pack-ice, and probably none do so in winter, so the southern limit of permanent ice is a realistic approximate northern boundary for belugas. Water temperatures encountered by belugas vary seasonally, but are usually below 59°F (15°C) and may be near to 32°F (0°C) for much of the year.

In belugas, as in many other creatures, seasonal variation in climate and habitat necessitates migration. For most populations, movements are driven by the fact that much of the Arctic is covered in an unbroken blanket of ice in winter.

Migrations range in scale dramatically. Belugas in the Gulf of St Lawrence, Canada, and the White Sea, Russia, probably just move seasonally from one part of the area to another, a distance of a few hundred miles. At the other extreme, belugas which summer in the western Canadian Arctic travel over 1,250 miles (2,000 km) to reach the area, only to be forced to leave again three months later as ice re-covers the region. Despite the great distances involved, there is no doubt of the animals' strong desire to reach this and other high latitude areas as soon as possible; belugas can travel for days on end at average speeds of 2 miles (3 km) per hour.

A pod of white whales passes through a 'lead' or crack in sea ice during early summer, taking advantage of the first chance to reach feeding areas which have been ice-covered since last freeze-up.

In spring and early summer, as the ice begins to crack and break up after the freezing embrace of winter, belugas can be seen pushing as far into the new cracks or 'leads' as they can. They seem impatient to reach their traditional summer grounds – areas of water that are covered by ice for all but a few short months, usually July-September. At the end of this period they progressively retreat ahead of the new autumnal freeze-up, to areas which remain essentially ice-free throughout the winter.

An obvious question is why do belugas migrate at all? Why not stay in warmer waters year-round? The answer is probably very simple: food. This, after all, is what attracts countless millions of migrating seabirds to nest in the Arctic. Despite their frigid temperatures, Arctic waters are very fertile in summer and

A bad error, but not necessarily a fatal one. Having become stranded by the falling tide,
this whale had to wait 10 hours before it could swim away.

hold huge concentrations of both vertebrate and invertebrate animals which form the prey of marine predators such as birds, seals, walruses and whales. Of course, food is available elsewhere, but a species able to survive where others cannot has a competitive advantage. It is only in the last few years, with the aid of modern research tools such as radio telemetry, that we have realized just how extraordinary is the beluga's ability to exploit resources out of the reach of other predators.

On their summer grounds, most belugas occupy areas of fresh water for periods varying from a few hours to days or even weeks. These areas differ greatly in size from the outlet of streams holding a few animals up to enormous estuarine deltas like that of the great Mackenzie River in north-west Canada, which covers many hundreds of square miles. The reasons for belugas seeking out fresh water seem complex. Firstly, as we have seen, it may play a role in skin molt. Secondly, the water here, though still very cold, is usually warmer than that offshore and the difference may be beneficial to calves which have mostly been born a little earlier. Thirdly, there may be an important social function involved here. An observer at these sites cannot fail to be struck by the high level of social interaction apparent between whales. It is unlikely that mating is the objective because pregnancies are probably initiated before the whales gain access to these areas, but there may be other social functions to this activity which have yet to be revealed.

The ability to move freely between salt water and fresh water is one shared by very few other cetaceans. Furthermore, no other whale is as comfortable in very shallow water. It is astounding to watch belugas deliberately swimming into water so shallow that they are effectively grounded, and it is this behavior which has allowed us to capture and release so many in our studies of migration. Though most belugas return safely to deeper water, there are problems other than zoologists to be wary of. Whales are sometimes cut off by falling tides and may suffer dehydration and skin damage before being rescued by the next high water. Worse, polar bears sometimes prowl in search of stranded belugas, or even attempt to grab them as they swim past in shallow water. This is relatively rare, but a group of polar bears were recently disturbed while beginning to feed on some unfortunate and very much alive belugas and narwhals that had been trapped by the receding tide in an estuary on Somerset Island. Not all stranded whales perish, though. Three radio-tagged belugas that were caught out by the tides in Cunningham Inlet all swam away 12 hours later and outlived the battery life of their tags, swimming many hundreds of miles in the process.

Belugas occur in the waters of all northern hemisphere states whose coastal peoples are familiar with sea ice: Norway, Russia, Alaska, Canada and Greenland. Occasionally lone, and probably lost, individuals turn up unexpectedly in places far removed from their usual range. A flurry of excited reports to my office recently marked the appearance of a white whale near the new Skye bridge in western Scotland, and others have been seen in western Europe over a period of years. Most spectacularly, a male called 'Brightness' is now free in the Black Sea and is apparently sometimes seen among schools of dolphins, having escaped from a Russian holding pool at Sevastopol during a storm. Its survival demonstrates that the species can adapt to far warmer waters than normal if required to.

All belugas, wherever they occur, are considered to be of one and the same species. Nevertheless, there are regional differences, particularly in body size, which demonstrate that many discrete populations of animals exist. In a few cases, our knowledge of the seasonal occurrence and migration of belugas in a particular area explains why they are isolated. This is particularly true for the animals in the St Lawrence Estuary in eastern Canada which rarely, if ever, stray outside the St Lawrence and are many hundreds of miles from any other belugas. In most cases, though, population boundaries are inferred (e.g. by body size differences), guessed at, or are a complete mystery. Hence, the number of different beluga populations remains open to doubt, and will be so until more

Resembling tears, mucous protects the vulnerable eye of this young whale from the damaging effects of drying after it became stranded. With help from the team of researchers that happened to be nearby, the whale swam off strongly on the next tide. The small hole behind the eye leads to the internal ear.

information on migrations and genetics is available from researchers. Some say that 18 different populations exist, while others recognize only 12. Clearly, we still have a lot yet to learn.

What does it matter, you may ask, how many populations can be distinguished? Why should scientists spend time and money trying to unlock the secrets of a harmless creature living in some of the most remote and inhospitable parts of our planet? The answer, sadly, is that man has already wiped out one of these unique groups of whales (in northern Quebec) and only an improved understanding of the others will put us in a position to prevent this happening again. Effective and safe management of belugas subjected to hunting by man, as in waterfowl, deer and other target species, is dependent on knowledge of the animal and its abundance. We shall be taking a closer look at the history and current status of beluga hunting, and other less obvious threats from man, in a later chapter.

Current estimates of the number of belugas in the world are very hazy. We are fairly confident of the size of some of the smaller and better studied populations, such as the one in the St Lawrence (it's likely to be between 500 and 1,000 animals), but the larger ones are difficult to count. Some are known to be in the order of tens of thousands, while others remain a mystery. In light of current knowledge, the total number is probably in the region of 100,000 to 200,000, but it would not be surprising if this figure has to be revised upwards as new information becomes available. This may sound like a lot of whales, but it means that there are fewer belugas in the world than there are people in even one medium-sized city, and they are spread over an area larger than the whole of Europe or North America.

On migration, belugas often travel in groups and close to the shoreline.
They can be hard to spot from the air.

Making a Living

As dwellers of a two-dimensional world, the land surface, it is difficult for us to understand or appreciate what it must be like to live in three dimensions as do marine mammals like the beluga. It is also tempting to think of seals and whales as animals which dive from, and return to, the sea surface. In reality, it is more appropriate to think of them as creatures of the deep ocean which rise to the surface for air, then return to the depths. They should therefore be more accurately described as 'surfacing' mammals rather than 'diving' ones.

Another difference between our world and that of the beluga is how information is gathered. We rely on our eyes, ears and nose to passively pick up information about our surroundings using light, sound and smell. In the sea, little light penetrates below about 300 ft (100 m), especially under ice, so eyes have little use in the deep ocean. Furthermore, many beluga populations winter in latitudes so far north that there is little or no daylight for a period of many months, so any animal relying on sight to find prey would surely starve. Chemical signals are transmitted by water and can be 'tasted' but, like air-borne smells, it is difficult to localize the exact source of the signal. However, water, being denser than air, carries sound clearly over long distances, and it is sound which cetaceans have adapted to use as their main source of environmental information. Rather than rely on purely passive listening, though, the toothed whales have developed a means of transmitting and receiving sound, called echolocation, which is similar to the 'sonar' of bats. It is so finely tuned that dolphins and whales can find objects and even 'see' what is inside them when blindfolded. In this way, fish can be found, chased and captured in complete darkness. Objects such as nets can be avoided no matter how murky the water. Furthermore, sound is the major way of communicating with other members of a group, of detecting the presence of predators and of establishing the direction of a beach or headland using the characteristic signature of breaking waves.

Each type of whale and dolphin has echolocation skills adapted to its own environment. Belugas are no exception, in that they have two skills which are particularly useful in ice-covered seas. They are unusually good at picking out low 'signal' levels in an otherwise noisy environment, and they seem to be able to use sound signals 'bounced' off the sea surface rather than arriving directly from the source. Unlike many dolphins, they also seem to be able to increase the resolution of sound information arriving by both sending and receiving sound simultaneously.

To our ears, listening to belugas through an underwater microphone, their communication and echolocation sounds seem to be a bewildering mixture of groans, buzzes, clicks, whistles, pops, 'raspberries' and myriad other noises. I well remember sitting in the little research hut above Cunningham Inlet listening enthralled to an indescribable cacophony of sounds being picked up by a hydrophone just off the beach below. Several times, inquisitive belugas could be seen swimming slowly up to the hydrophone itself, investigating it by sound. The little hut reverberated to rapid click-sequences sounding like a creaky door hinge, becoming deafening as the animal almost touched the sensor, before turning away in search of something more animated than a black lump on the end of a rubber-coated cable.

Belugas are probably the most vocal of all cetaceans, and were dubbed 'sea-canaries' by mariners familiar with their sounds penetrating the drum-like hull of a ship. Their uniqueness is even better exemplified by the noise they make *above* water. Some nights at Cunningham Inlet I was unable to sleep because of the extraordinary noises emanating from perhaps 500 belugas playing and scratching in the river outlet below. Passing air through the 'lips' of their blowhole, the whales could blow 'raspberries', whistle and scream over large distances. Combined with a great deal of splashing using tails and heads, the effect was at the same time both amusing and awe-inspiring; one of those experiences that can never be forgotten.

Although belugas possess a remarkable range of vocal communication, they are not renowned for spectacular above-water behavior as are, for example, humpback

The trailing edge of the tail becomes increasingly curvaceous with age.
The dark edge to this one suggests that the whale is not yet fully mature.

whales and many marine dolphins. Certainly neither I, nor anyone I know, have ever seen a beluga leap completely clear of the water in the wild. An exception to this rather sober existence can occur during the short period of time most belugas spend in estuaries each summer. By no means all shrug off their inhibitions, but those in Cunningham Inlet certainly seem to do so, at least by their standards. Heads, tails and flippers are repeatedly slapped against the water surface, sending great plumes of water into the air. Animals spy-hop (stand vertically with their heads clear of the water) and others move slowly around with their head raised at 45 degrees. Groups may even flail against the current in shallow fast-running streams, resembling large fat salmon more than whales.

As in all wild animals, the hunt for food is a major occupation for belugas. Until recently, it was thought that they were exclusively shallow-water animals, and that their food was therefore found coastally. One of the most exciting discoveries of radio telemetry research in recent years is that this assumption was very much mistaken. In fact, although food is sometimes taken while belugas are in coastal waters, it seems that most, at least in summer, is taken on the seabed in depths of up to 1,800 ft (550 m). A typical feeding dive requires the whale to hold its breath for 12-20 minutes. The larger males have an advantage in this respect over females and juveniles, allowing them to feed in deeper waters and to spend a larger proportion of time foraging on the seabed. For one population at least, the one which spends the summer in the Beaufort Sea north of Alaska and western Canada, different diving abilities between the sexes may explain why they segregate in late July and August. Having migrated eastwards with the females along the north coast of Alaska and reached the Mackenzie delta, the adult males turn sharply northwards and head to Viscount Melville Sound, more than 500 miles (800 km) away. Here they feed at a 'restaurant' which excludes the ladies simply because it's in a deep trench on the sea floor which only the largest whales have the breath-hold capacity to reach.

During a feeding dive, the whale invariably swims straight down to the seabed, remains for 5-10 minutes on the bottom, then returns at a similar speed to the surface. The journeys to and from the seabed are not used for feeding. On the seabed, belugas swim very slowly. They may be sifting the silt or sand for invertebrates like worms, or they may be using a stealthy fishing technique; perhaps allowing mobile fish to approach them, or surprising non-mobile fish like halibut on the sea floor.

Seabed-dwelling invertebrate prey has been found in the stomachs of hunter-killed belugas. Another pointer to a life spent snuffling around for food on the sea floor is the fact that beluga teeth are often worn, sometimes to the gumline. This characteristic is common in other animals which forage for invertebrates in a silty or sandy habitat, such as the walrus, but is rare in sea mammals which eat just midwater fish and squid.

Visitors to the aquaria where belugas are kept in captivity have probably noticed how the shape of their mouth can be changed in a similar way to ourselves – an ability not shared with any other whale. They may also have noticed how belugas can squirt jets of water very accurately with their mouths. How and why have these characteristics evolved? My guess is that they are used in feeding. A jet of water could be a very useful tool for blowing away silt in the search for hidden prey such as worms or sandeels. Testing this hypothesis will probably have to wait until we can persuade a beluga to carry a camera down to the depths and film itself feeding. This may sound far-fetched, but researchers are currently developing a pressure-proofed miniature camera which is intended exactly for this purpose.

Although seabed invertebrates seem likely, on the basis of circumstantial evidence, to be a significant part of the beluga diet, fish are likely to be the most important prey throughout most of their range. Examination of the contents of the stomachs of harvested belugas in several areas has demonstrated a fondness for a variety of fish, most of them probably caught at depth. Commonly taken are capelin, halibut, lantern fish, redfish and members of the cod family. The polar cod, a relatively small fish which often forms huge schools, is particularly important and is

Spyhopping. Head and shoulders out of the water, these whales are taking a good look at what's happening around Cunningham Inlet.

Feeding dives typically last 12–20 minutes and are usually made right down to the seabed.

the dominant food in some areas. This has been strikingly demonstrated several times along the south coast of Devon Island in the Canadian Arctic archipelago, Here, polar cod schools hundreds of yards in length and holding thousands of tons of fish may suddenly appear in the shallows just off the beach, perhaps in a vain attempt to escape from underwater predators. These schools, resembling a long, sinuous oil-slick from above, attract enormous numbers of fish-eaters which gorge themselves until every last cod has been consumed. From above, the fish are attacked by fulmars, kittiwakes and guillemots. From below, they face the onslaught of harp seals, ringed seals, narwhals and often many hundreds of belugas. The banquet may last several days, after which the satiated belugas disperse and would be lucky indeed to find another such easy meal in the same season.

Resembling a sinuous oil slick, this huge school of fish provides a long-lasting feast for belugas and other predators.

The amount of food required by a wild beluga has never been measured, but we can estimate it from the amount consumed by captive animals. A beluga in an aquarium eats between about 1% and 5% of its own body weight in fish every day, depending on its size; smaller whales eat proportionally more than larger ones. Wild animals live in colder water and are more active, so they are likely to eat more than this, but we can use 1% as a conservative estimate for adults. An average-sized beluga of, say, 1,540 lb (700 kg) bodyweight will therefore eat about 15 lb (7 kg) of fish per day, and 2.5 tons per year. A population of 10,000 animals would then eat 25,000 tons in a year, so it's clear that whatever they feed on, be it fish or invertebrates, must be extremely abundant. What is it that occurs in such quantities on the floor of the deep Arctic Ocean trenches that belugas find so attractive? This is an intriguing mystery, and one to which we may soon have the answer.

Because the aim of a feeding dive is to spend as much time as possible where the food is, i.e. on the seabed, belugas use their breath-hold capacity as

economically as possible. This means descending and ascending at an optimum speed (not too fast or too slow) and beginning the ascent at the time necessary to allow surfacing when almost all on-board oxygen supplies have been depleted. We have recently discovered that the optimum speed for diving in belugas is around 4-7 ft (1-2 m) per second, which is a slow jogging speed for us. Deep dives normally last 12-20 minutes, but can exceptionally be extended to 25 minutes. Deep foraging dives tend to be carried out in bouts rather than individually and an adult beluga typically needs about five minutes at the surface to recover from a 15-minute dive. It therefore can spend about 75% of its time underwater during such bouts. This is a similar performance to that of other cetaceans, but doesn't come near that of elephant seals which can manage with just two minutes at the surface after an hour under water!

Moving through water uses energy and oxygen. A beluga must gain its energy through feeding and, being an air-breather, must visit the sea surface to exchange its stale air for a new supply periodically. The various types of whale and dolphin have evolved different ways of keeping themselves adequately supplied with oxygen, which allows them to 'burn' energy for swimming. At one extreme,

small shallow-water feeders like the Amazon river dolphin, or boto, breathe only once each time they approach the surface, then dive for a minute or two. At the other, large deep-water feeders, like the sperm whale, take 40 or 50 breaths during one surfacing period, then can submerge for an hour or more. Belugas tend to follow the boto strategy while in shallow water or swimming near the surface, but switch to something similar to the sperm whale technique when feeding on the seabed in deep water.

Adult belugas are seemingly effortless swimmers, but young calves are weak and inexperienced, and have great difficulty keeping up with their mothers unaided. They soon learn to overcome this problem by getting a 'tow', simply by positioning themselves very close to the mother's body behind the dorsal ridge and getting an assisted ride like that of a wild goose flying behind the leader in a 'V' formation.

A fascinating question is how belugas find places to breathe when swimming under sea ice. A mistake made here is likely to be the whale's final one, and the readiness with which this species ventures under ice suggests that it is well able to detect potential breathing sites. Some recent results of our satellite telemetry work in the Beaufort Sea may indicate how this is done. We noticed that whales traveling over a particular stretch of water early in the season made a series of extremely deep 'V' shaped dives lasting up to 25 minutes, some to as much as 3,300 ft (1,000 m). On their return across the same stretch of water a month later, they remained near the surface. Inspection of ice maps showed that this part of the Beaufort was completely covered with ice during the outward journey and ice-free on the return. Furthermore, these deep dives were quite unlike anything that we had seen in the records of any other belugas. Could it be that the whales were diving down to allow them to search the ice ceiling for holes in much the same way as a pilot of an aircraft uses altitude to provide the best chance of finding an emergency landing site? If so, belugas must somehow be able to see or hear such holes at distances of half a mile or more. Such an ability would be extraordinary, but perhaps not beyond the sensory acuity of a species so beautifully adapted to this environment.

The Arctic is a harsh and unforgiving place to live, and to die. Despite their extraordinary diving
and sensory capabilities, this group of belugas was cut off by the rapid formation of new ice as the short summer ended,
before they could migrate to safety. As their pool of open water grew ever smaller, they became progressively thinner
and lost their bright white color. Nothing could be done to save them.

Getting Close

Cetaceans have been on captive display since the late 18th century, when a few dolphins were kept in tiny pools and provided an intrigued public with the first glimpse of these exotic animals. In those days there was little expertise available in how to care for these creatures, and they soon perished. The idea really caught on during the 1950s with the establishment of purpose-built marine parks, made possible by advances in marine mammal husbandry and the resultant ability to keep animals alive for years and even breed them successfully. Dolphins proved to be extremely popular with the public, and their image was enhanced with TV documentaries and the famous 'Flipper' shows. Instead of being animals to exploit for meat, oil and industrial products, cetaceans quickly became perceived as gentle, intelligent creatures, worth preserving in their own right. Belugas were appealing and proved to be relatively adaptable to captivity; they became one of the most commonly held species and are today maintained in many facilities across Europe, North America and Japan. Almost all were captured as juveniles from Churchill, Canada, where a major concentration of belugas occurs every summer within a few miles of an airport and immediate access to the cities of Canada and the United States. For many years, Churchill residents had hunted belugas to kill them; they had to develop new hunting techniques to capture the whales alive and unharmed.

More recently, Canada has granted few permits to allow further live captures, but calves are being born in captivity and the world's aquaria may soon become self-sufficient in this respect.

Besides public display, belugas have been held in confinement for another, less publicized and to many a more sinister reason. The navies of both the United States and the former Soviet Union saw in this species a trainable animal which could perhaps be put to work in the service of the respective state. Many details of this secret work are of course not made public, but we know that it explored the use of the beluga's remarkable diving ability in the deployment and retrieval of armaments, and in relation to the work of submarines. In addition to military work, the U. S. Navy facilities were, and are, used to conduct some of the best research into cetacean physiology, in particular the mechanics and energetics of diving and swimming. Foremost in this field is Dr Sam Ridgway, who pioneered studies of the diving capabilities of belugas and bottlenose dolphins using animals trained to perform tasks such as pushing buttons on submerged equipment at various depths. Among other things, these buttons could be used to trigger a photograph of the diving animal. I well remember being stunned at one such photograph which showed a dolphin with a great cavity in the side of its chest. Here was dramatic proof that the lungs and rib-cages of cetaceans have evolved to collapse as the animal swims down, thereby avoiding damage to the ribs and diaphragm that our own species, for example, would suffer in the same circumstances. Of course, the thoracic collapse is reversible; as the diving animal nears the surface the reducing water pressure allows air in the lungs to re-expand, so it breaks the surface looking normal. Captive animals also offer the civilian researcher opportunities which are unavailable in the wild. Much of our knowledge of the physiology, health, reproduction, behavior and nutrition of small cetaceans has derived from studies of animals in pools rather than the open sea.

Unsurprisingly, there is another side to this apparently rosy picture. The process of capture, transportation and confinement in an unnaturally small and shallow space must be extremely traumatic to a sentient animal raised in the wild. Some die in the early stages of this process. Others, while surviving, show behavioral abnormalities consistent with stress for the rest of their lives. There is, though, no doubt that progress is being made in the way cetaceans are kept and displayed. Increased experience and research has led to better-fed, healthier animals which are housed in larger pools. Training regimes are

*Belugas in captivity. Facilities such as this one allow millions of people to see belugas
up close for the first, and perhaps only, time. Furthermore, much of our knowledge of small cetaceans
derives from studies of captive animals. Now, though, society is asking itself whether the keeping of whales
and dolphins is morally justifiable, whatever the benefits may be.*

increasingly designed to keep both the watcher and the watched entertained, so reducing the incidence of stress disorders. Nevertheless, captive conditions can never truly mimic the wild. Having learned how to keep small cetaceans alive, society is now asking whether the confinement of cetaceans, or indeed any wild animal, is justifiable. Pending a resolution of the debate on the principle of captive display, few would argue with the current trend to improve or shut down the remaining facilities in which cetaceans are clearly stressed or ill-treated.

If seeing belugas in captivity is not possible or not enough for you, modern air travel has now brought the realm of the wild beluga within reach of millions of ordinary people. No longer do you need to be a polar explorer to see white whales in their natural habitat! By far the easiest and cheapest places to aim for, even for those living as far away as Europe, are in Canada. Two areas stand out as offering the highest chance of seeing belugas at close quarters for a reasonable cost: Churchill on Hudson's Bay, and the western Gulf of St Lawrence near the mouth of the Saguenay River. Both are well south of the Arctic circle and have facilities to both accommodate tourists and take them on the water to see whales. The more adventurous traveler can find belugas in Svalbard, Russia, Alaska, Arctic Canada and Greenland, but usually with less predictability and at a greater cost. Churchill will be familiar to many as the 'polar bear capital of the world', where hundreds of these magnificent creatures gather on the shores of Hudson's Bay in late autumn, waiting for it to refreeze . A little earlier, in July and August, belugas gather in large numbers in the lower reaches of the Churchill River, at the edge of town. They can be seen from the riverbank and from the port, but it is better still to book a trip on the river and get really close to them. With luck, some will even follow the boat, although the tea-colored water doesn't allow much to be seen more than about 3 ft (1 m) below the water surface. The great thing about this site is that the belugas are extremely reliable; it would be difficult to spend a few days in Churchill at the right time of year without seeing them to your heart's content.

Tail of a sub-adult.

The beluga population in the Gulf of St Lawrence is much smaller than that of Hudson's Bay, but it too concentrates in a few accessible locations in summer. The best area to visit is near the town of Tadoussac, where the Saguenay River meets the St Lawrence. Here, belugas can be seen both from land and from the water. Vessel operators are not permitted to specifically seek out and approach belugas because of the risk of harassment, but the animals are tolerant of traffic and can routinely be seen from ferries or boats taking tourists out to see other whale species.

Seeing belugas in the wild is now becoming increasingly popular, and provides an experience that no-one will forget.

Belugas and Man

For millions of years belugas or their direct ancestors have lived on this planet with little threat to them other than from the harsh environment to which they have become adapted. Then, some 3,000 years ago, a mere blink of an eye in relation to this timescale, things began to change. Waves of human migration had by then brought two-legged predators into the pristine Arctic marine environment for the first time. Initially, the small number of people and their primitive hunting techniques had little impact on marine mammal populations; predator and prey co-existing in a way that could probably have been sustained indefinitely. Then, in much more recent times, this harmonious balance was first threatened, then cast aside. Advancing technology and an increasing human population in Europe brought about another wave of migration to the Arctic, this time in search of wealth in the form of animal and mineral resources. Whales, seals, walruses and birds were ruthlessly killed with no thought to the future. Steller's sea cow, a large relative of the manatee, and the great auk were completely exterminated within a frighteningly short space of time. The bowhead whale, a once-common resident of the very same waters occupied by belugas, was mercilessly hunted and killed for its oil-laden blubber and its enormously long baleen plates. Whalers only left it alone when it, too, had been rendered almost extinct. Being relatively small, belugas escaped the worst ravages of European whalers until about a century ago when bowhead stocks had all but disappeared. Then, perhaps out of frustration and to fill otherwise empty oil barrels, some large beluga kills were made. At Elwin Bay, a shallow inlet on Canada's Somerset Island, some 10,000 belugas were taken by Scottish whalers between 1874 and 1898. They employed the simple technique of driving whales into the Bay at high water, creating a lot of noise at the mouth as the tide receded to prevent an escape, then killing and processing the stranded animals at low tide. Literally hundreds of belugas could thus be taken in a single day, and the whalers exhausted themselves in the process. One Captain wrote, 'This is terrible work. I have not been in my bed in 17 days and our ship is in great danger of being driven ashore at any time. The Black whaling (for bowhead whales) is bad enough, but this is one thousand times worse.' The bones of these animals lie bleached and untouched on the beach around the Bay to this day, an eerie reminder of the destructive power of man.

In Svalbard, to the north of Norway, commercial whalers took large numbers of belugas until as recently as 1955. In Churchill, Manitoba, a hunt was maintained until 1968 and the rusting machinery once used for oil and meat production is still in place.

The impact of such an explosive increase in hunting was predictable. Although no populations were totally destroyed, many were dramatically reduced in size. Meanwhile, and especially in this century, beluga harvests by the native Inuit continued and often increased as motor-powered boats and rifles replaced skin-covered craft and hand-thrown harpoons. Some whale populations, already heavily depleted by commercial hunting, such as those in the fjords of Baffin Island, were pushed even closer to extinction. Others, like the one which summers around Somerset Island in the eastern Canadian Arctic and winters in northern Baffin Bay between Canada and Greenland, continue to sustain Inuit harvests which are in themselves large and probably beyond the endurable capacity of the beluga population. It is likely that no population has escaped hunting at some time and several may never recover from it because so few animals remain.

As if all this wasn't enough, man's burgeoning population and his technological advance have resulted in other less obvious pressures on the unfortunate beluga. Along Alaska's northern coastline, and in adjacent Canadian waters, the hunt for oil has resulted in the construction of noisy artificial islands and causeways right on the migration path of the Beaufort Sea beluga population. In eastern Canada, ice-breaking ships coming to carry away lead/zinc ore from mines in the Lancaster Sound region have been shown to cause panic in belugas as much as 50 miles (80 km) away. In the St Lawrence it's a miracle any belugas survive. Following large-scale hunting, the population was subjected to bombing and culling to protect fisheries, had its traditionally used estuaries ruined by hydro-electric power schemes and is now suffering health problems, perhaps linked to the appalling industrial pollution poured daily into its habitat.

Faced with this catalog of historical and continuing abuse, what future can we expect for the beluga? The good news is that, in common with many wild animals, the beluga is remarkably resilient. Most populations have survived the worst ravages of hunting and some show signs of recovering. Others, such as the one which passes through the Mackenzie delta in north-west Canada, are large enough to sustain indefinitely the modest harvest taken each year by native peoples. In north-west Greenland, recognition that the current level of Inuit hunt cannot be sustained at present levels has occurred early enough to allow remedial action before it is too late.

Not all interactions with man are harmful. Tagging studies (as here on a beluga that became stranded by the falling tide) are providing information to help conserve the species.

The bad news is that the eleventh hour has been reached for some populations. In Cumberland Sound, south-east Baffin Island, the continuing hunt on a population heavily depleted by commercial whaling is likely to be greater than the recruitment of young animals each year. Sadly, because of misunderstandings and cultural clashes between the Inuit hunters and government wildlife managers, there is resistance to hunting controls which might allow a recovery. Just a little south, at Ungava Bay in northern Quebec, it is already too late. This once buoyant population is effectively extinct.

Meat and blubber dries on a rack made of driftwood on the shore of the Beaufort Sea, Canada.
In many Inuit communities, beluga hunting is an important means of providing both food and a sense of cultural identity.

It is very easy for those of us living comfortably in modern western societies to decry the hunting of wild animals for food. But many human societies in the past, and some to this day, have relied on belugas for their food in much the same way as we rely on farm-produced livestock. One such group of people is the Inuvialuit of the Arctic coast of north-west Canada. Every summer, groups of hunters from local villages and towns venture out to traditional camping sites on the seaward edge of the Mackenzie delta to take a small number of belugas (usually one to four) for their families' and friends' needs during the year. The hunt is carefully monitored, and care is taken to ensure that the total removals from the population (currently around 150 per year) can be sustained without depleting its size. The most prized part of the whale is the skin, called muktuk, which is usually eaten in small chunks, either raw, boiled or smoked. Meat is cut into strips and sun-dried on wooden racks for storage. The hunt is a source of community pride and cultural identity

which is passed from generation to generation. Although the sight of whales being killed would shock most onlookers from Europe or North America, much of that reaction would be due to the way we have become insulated from the methods used to produce meat for our own tables. From that standpoint, it is difficult to criticize a sustainable native whale hunt without being hypocritical. Nevertheless, it would surely be wrong to stand idly by and watch others repeat the mistakes of our own ancestors who, through ignorance, wiped out many prey species. Today's knowledge and resources, employed and shared wisely, can and should help prevent such a fate falling on the beluga.

One final topic should be mentioned in relation to the future of belugas; that of climate change. Climatologists confidently predict that the Arctic will warm by

several degrees Fahrenheit over the next 50-100 years, partly because of the huge recent production of 'greenhouse' gases. This would result in a substantial melting of sea ice and the likelihood that most of the beluga's range, currently protected from direct harm by man because of the ice cover, will rapidly be subjected to ship traffic, oil exploitation and all the environmental problems these bring. For those familiar with the Arctic, the removal of much of its white safety blanket is a disturbing prospect, especially if this profound change is brought about by our own wasteful use of fossil fuels. The overall effect of global warming on belugas is not yet certain, but all the signs suggest that it will be damaging. If the sea ice edge retreats beyond the edge of the continental shelf of the Old and New Worlds, and if belugas are as reliant on its ecological community as we believe, then the consequences could be very serious for this little whale.

It would be a mistake to write off an animal that has already survived climate change, habitat degradation, centuries of hunting and some of the planet's most hostile conditions. But we must be vigilant, for it seems that the future wellbeing of this enigmatic creature may well rest in our own hands.

Beluga Whale Facts

Common names:	Beluga, white whale
Scientific name:	*Delphinapterus leucas*
Geographical range:	Arctic waters of USA, Canada, Greenland, Norway, Russia

Adult body size (males are bigger than females in the same population)

Length:	Typically – 10-15 ft (3-4.5 m)
	Maximum – 18 ft (5.5 m)
Weight:	Typically – 900-2,275 lb (400-1,030 kg)
	Maximum – 2 tons
Length at birth:	4.6-5.3 ft (1.4-1.6 m)
Color:	dark gray-brown at birth, becoming lighter with age and only white in adulthood
Longevity:	up to 30 years of age, exceptionally 40

Recommended Reading

The first three titles below provide a broad and readable discussion of cetaceans as a group. The last has a detailed chapter on the white whale.

Whales and Dolphins by Anthony Martin and a team of experts, Salamander Books (UK) and Random House (US), 1990, *The Ecology of Whales and Dolphins* by D. E. Gaskin, Heinemann, 1982, *The Natural History of Whales and Dolphins* by Peter Evans, Christopher Helm (Publishers), 1987, *Handbook of Marine Mammals,* Vol 4, edited by Sam H Ridgway and Sir Richard Harrison, Academic Press, 1989.

Biographical Note

Anthony Martin has been a cetacean biologist with the UK's Cambridge-based Sea Mammal Research Unit since 1978. During this time he has studied whales, dolphins and porpoises in many parts of the world and feels most at home in small, remote fieldcamps with dolphins on his doorstep. Tony's current fieldwork migrations take him to the Arctic in summer and the Amazon in winter. A delegate to the Scientific Committee of the International Whaling Commission for 18 years, Tony now chairs its work on small cetaceans. This is his fourth book.

Tony Martin gratefully acknowledges the colleagues and friends of many nationalities who have contributed to joint research work mentioned in this book.